SPEECH, LANGUAGE & COMMUNICATION
Pocketbook

By Victoria Mason &
Emela Milne

SLCN

Published by:

Teachers' Pocketbooks
Laurel House, Station Approach,
Alresford, Hampshire SO24 9JH, UK
Tel: +44 (0)1962 735573
Fax: +44 (0)1962 733637
Email: sales@teacherspocketbooks.co.uk
Website: www.teacherspocketbooks.co.uk

Teachers' Pocketbooks is an imprint of
Management Pocketbooks Ltd.

Series editor – Linda Edge

This edition published 2014
ISBN 978 1 906610 70 8

E-book ISBN 978 1 908284 70 9

British Library Cataloguing-in-Publication Data
– A catalogue record for this book is available
from the British Library.

Design, artwork and graphics by Efex Ltd.
Printed in UK.

Contents

Foreword

'The ability to communicate is an essential life skill for all children and young people and it underpins a child's social, emotional and educational development. Strong language and communication skills are linked to better outcomes for children and young people in school and beyond'. **(The Communication Trust, 2012)**

Effective speech, language and communication skills are essential not only in the arenas of education and work, but for all types of formal and informal social interactions. For the majority, these skills are instinctive and we barely give them a second thought.

However, in most of our classes there will be some children who haven't acquired these fundamental skills and who will need help to develop them. Recent research has estimated that in an average school classroom at least 10% of pupils are likely to have persistent, long-term speech, language or communication needs, with upwards of 50% of children in some areas having delayed language skills. These children can face huge obstacles in school, academically, socially and behaviourally.

Foreword

This book is written primarily for mainstream school staff and is particularly useful for anybody working with or managing pupils with SLCN (speech, language and communication needs), including teachers, senior management, SENCOs, teaching assistants, pastoral staff, trainee teachers and support staff.

Throughout our careers in schools – as a teacher and speech and language therapist – we have worked with many students with SLCN and in this book share with you our experience and the support strategies we have used successfully in mainstream classrooms.

We hope that this book will develop your expertise in supporting pupils with speech, language and communication needs. By learning techniques that will improve their ability to communicate, your students will gain independence and confidence and you can empower them to achieve academically and participate socially.

Foreword

The first section of this book gives an overview of SLCN and is followed by sections looking at specific areas of difficulty in the classroom. You'll learn how to recognise the difficulties pupils encounter as a result of SLCN and how to enable them to access the school curriculum with increased independence.

Speech, language and communication is a vast topic. It overlaps with many different disciplines, from psychology, sociology and linguistics, to education and health. A book of this size cannot provide a comprehensive insight into every aspect of SLCN; what it can do is focus on the 'need-to-knows' for busy school staff – the practical tips that can make a big difference in the classroom.

You'll find links to further reading, training and resources at the end of the book, and if you'd like to know more about literacy acquisition, the *Literacy Across the Curriculum* and *Dyslexia* Pocketbooks are also available in this series.

Introduction to SLCN

 Attention and Listening

 Understanding Language

 Speech

 Using Language

 Vocabulary

 Social Communication

 A Whole School Approach

Introduction to SLCN

What is SLCN?

So, let's start at the beginning. What exactly does the term SLCN encompass?

Speech is the ability to articulate sounds and use them correctly within words. It also refers to fluency and clarity – to our voice quality and intonation, and the way we use expression to convey and support meaning.

Language is the system and rules which govern the way we assemble words to create sentences, conversations and longer narratives. It refers both to the ability to construct language and to make sense of it.

Communication is intentional interaction between people, both verbal and non-verbal. It includes using language for different purposes; listening and social skills; expressing and understanding emotions; facial expression; tone of voice and body language.

Needs arise when difficulties with any of the above have an impact on a pupil's ability to interact with others at an appropriate level for their age.

Typical development – early years

Most children acquire speech, language and communication skills instinctively, a process that begins at birth and continues into adulthood. Children develop language at different rates but some typical milestones are:

8-20 weeks. Infants begin to coo and laugh. They recognise the sounds that belong to their 'mother tongue', the language they have been listening to in the womb.

25 weeks – 1 year. As babies interact with their world they associate sound sequences with objects they feel and see. They develop understanding of interaction through eye contact, copying and turn-taking. These precede first attempts to say recognisable words which begin with babbling (nananana, adah-adah) and 'nonsense' words (geg, ada).

1 year onwards. Understand simple instructions with visual clues. Begin to use first words with meaning, although sounds may not be correct. Understand that language and communication have a purpose.

Typical development – early years

18 months. Vocabulary of approximately 5-20 words, mostly nouns.

2 years onwards. Roughly two thirds of what is said is intelligible, vocabulary of around 150-300 words, begin to use pronouns and prepositions.

3 years onwards. Begin to understand simple questions, vocabulary of around 900 words, start to create sentences.

4 years onwards. Much wider vocabulary, extensive talk while carrying out activities, speech almost entirely intelligible.

5 years onwards. Speech almost grammatically correct, use of longer sentences and joining sentences, increased vocabulary includes adjectives and adverbs.

Typical development – primary years

Children make huge progress with speech, language and communication skills at primary school.

Age	Listening and understanding	Vocabulary and grammar	Social interaction
4-5	• Look at who is speaking • Understand two- to three-part instructions • Begin to be able to answer 'how' and 'why' questions	• Group words and give examples *(Colours: red, blue, yellow)* • Sentences are understandable with some errors *(I felled down the stairs)*	• Start and take part in conversations • Pretend to be other people (make-believe) • Begin to discuss ideas and feelings
7-9	• Make relevant, comments which relate to what has been said • Identify when they haven't understood • Begin to be able to infer what isn't explicitly said	• Use regular and irregular word endings *(I walked, I went)* • Use more complex grammar accurately • Use topic vocabulary	• Begin to use formal language when appropriate • Take turns and learn other 'rules' of conversation • Begin to use tone of voice and gesture to help communicate

Typical development – secondary years

Children and young people continue to develop speech, language and communication skills through secondary school.

Age	Listening and understanding	Vocabulary and grammar	Social interaction
11	• Understand more complex directions • Understand factual information but might find inference difficult • Start to understand sarcasm	• Use a range of words to join sentences • Tell stories accurately and in sequence • Find academic instructions difficult *(eg estimate, research, define)*	• Understand jokes based on double meanings • Aware when not understood by others • Switch often between topics
18	• Understand a wide variety of topics • Ask for help in a specific way when haven't understood • Follow complex instructions	• Use a range of arguments to persuade others • Use range of descriptions and expressions • Tell long and complex narratives	• Stay on topic as required and move sensibly to other topics • Switch easily between formal and informal language • Repair 'breakdowns' in conversation

For more detailed information about what to expect at each age and stage of a child's development, see www.talkingpoint.org.uk

Who has SLCN?

Speech, language and communication difficulties affect a wide range of students. Some will have **delayed** language development, ie they will develop normally but more slowly than is typical. Others will have **disordered** language development. They may have a specific difficulty with one or more aspects of language.

- A pupil can have a specific speech, language or communication difficulty **without any other known disability**. Their cognitive and visual skills, and performance in physical or practical tasks may be within the average range
- For other pupils, SLCN may be **part of wider learning difficulties**. Those with moderate or severe learning difficulties, or with identified conditions such as Down's Syndrome, may struggle with many aspects of speech, language and communication
- Pupils with **Autistic Spectrum Conditions** (including Asperger syndrome) have particular difficulties with social communication skills and higher order language skills, such as inference and figurative language

Who else has SLCN?

- Children with **physical difficulties**, including motor coordination and cleft palate, may have particular problems with speech. Those with hearing difficulties can also struggle with language development

- Pupils who have suffered head injuries following accidents or illnesses such as meningitis, which affect how the brain works, may have **acquired difficulties**. In these cases a range of complex speech, language and communication needs can arise and pupils are often referred to specialist teams

- Looked after children and those in areas where a high proportion of families live in poverty are at risk of **social disadvantage**. An impoverished language environment and/ or limited language interactions give rise to SLCN. Such pupils are often initially identified because of difficulties with attention and listening

What about...?

Children with SLCN rarely fit neatly into boxes or text book descriptions. They often have overlapping difficulties or don't quite meet the criteria for a particular diagnosis. You may encounter SLCN in learners with selective talking, dyslexia and EAL.

Selective talking (or selective mutism) – students only talk in certain settings or with certain people.

Dyslexia – pupils may struggle with phonological awareness, early speech and vocabulary development, acquiring literacy, sequential memory and organisation.

EAL (English as an Additional Language) – EAL students who have difficulties in their first language, may also have SLCN in English.

Creating a language-friendly environment in your classroom will help all pupils, regardless of their 'label' and whether or not SLCN has been formally identified.

What's the problem?

50-90% of children with persistent SLCN go on to have reading difficulties.
(Dockerell, J., Every Child A Talker Conference 2010)

Two thirds of 7-14 year olds with serious behaviour problems had a language impairment.
(The Communication Trust, 2011)

Studies show that between 55-100% of pupils with social, emotional and behavioural difficulties have SLCN which has never been recognised.
(The Communication Trust, 2011)

Only 25% of pupils with SLCN achieve the expected level in English at the end of Key Stage 2 and 15% of pupils with SLCN achieve 5 A* – C GCSEs.
(from National Pupil Database quoted in Bercow Report, 2008)

What is the impact in school?

Language is the medium through which we teach content and skills; it is fundamental to learning and academic achievement. The most common ways of teaching and of assessing learning in schools are language based:

- Written tests and exams
- Written classwork, essays or homework
- Oral presentations
- Discussion and participation in class – either whole-class or group situations
- Listening to the teacher

Pupils with any aspect of SLCN will find it hard to show what they know. This will affect their academic achievement, participation, engagement and, ultimately, their confidence and self-esteem.

It's not just academic

SLCN is now recognised as also having a significant impact on social, emotional and behavioural development.

Social. Pupils with SLCN often find it hard to build and maintain friendships and to interact appropriately. They may be isolated, withdrawn or socially inappropriate.

Emotional. The ability to reflect on our feelings and emotions is essential in developing a sense of self. Being able to talk to others about this helps us to develop emotionally. It is often hard for children with speech and language difficulties to understand their emotions and to develop a sense of identity.

Behavioural. Learners with SLCN can find understanding and explaining events or incidents problematic. They sometimes get themselves or others into trouble for things they haven't done. If they see school as difficult or boring they are more likely to disengage or misbehave.

How language works

Understanding and using language (both spoken and written) is a complex process:

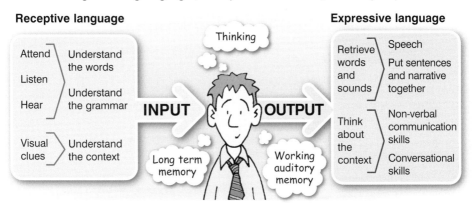

Reading and writing add extra levels of processing at the input and output stages respectively.

(Adapted from Hayden & Jordan, 2004 – see page 126)

Language and literacy

Inevitably, pupils with SLCN often have associated difficulties with literacy.

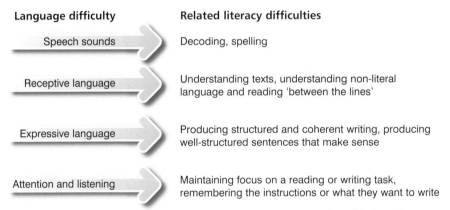

Language difficulty	Related literacy difficulties
Speech sounds	Decoding, spelling
Receptive language	Understanding texts, understanding non-literal language and reading 'between the lines'
Expressive language	Producing structured and coherent writing, producing well-structured sentences that make sense
Attention and listening	Maintaining focus on a reading or writing task, remembering the instructions or what they want to write

Time spent developing spoken language and communication skills will help with literacy acquisition and so improve access to the curriculum.

Why prioritise SLC skills in the classroom?

If pupils develop stronger speech, language and communication skills they will:

- Improve academic progress and achievement
- Become more engaged in lessons
- Have better social relations with their peers
- Be able to ask for help when they need it and communicate more effectively
- Be able to identify and discuss their emotions
- Have more confidence and self-esteem

As well as being vital for learning, speech, language and communication skills are essential across the school day, for pupils to make friends, sort out problems and share experiences.
(The Communication Trust, 2011)

Oral language skills such as vocabulary knowledge and storytelling skills have been shown to be strong predictors of academic success.
(Feinstein & Duckworth, 2006, Development in the Early Years: its importance for school performance and adult outcomes)

Top 5 things to remember

1. SLCN affects a large proportion of pupils in schools. Some difficulties are obvious; others (such as difficulties with receptive language) can be well hidden.
2. SLCN impacts on social and emotional wellbeing, behaviour and literacy, as well as academic achievement.
3. All children develop at a different rate, but not reaching typical milestones could indicate possible SLCN.
4. SLCN includes difficulties with speech, attention and listening, learning vocabulary, using language, understanding what is said, social communication and understanding concepts. Pupils may have difficulties in several areas.
5. Some pupils may have **delayed** language development; others may have **disordered** language development.

Attention and Listening

Attention span of a goldfish – 9 seconds

Remember the last time you struggled to focus in a meeting or lecture? There may have been several reasons:

The room was too hot or cold

You weren't interested

You felt unwell/ tired

You didn't understand

Chair was uncomfortable

There were interruptions

You couldn't hear

You were worried, stressed or anxious about something else

Physical discomfort, emotional distress and lack of motivation affect children's attention in the classroom in the same way.

We tend to over-estimate the average attention span of even normally developing children at the best of times. Experts estimate somewhere between 5 and 20 minutes depending on age, situation, interest, level and type of task, and time of day.

Listening and maintaining attention are key elements in communication and the basis of successful learning in the classroom.

Listening demands of the classroom

In a typical school day pupils are expected to:

- Listen to and follow instructions
- Understand oral descriptions and explanations
- Sustain attention for extended amounts of time
- Understand commentaries and speakers on video clips
- Follow and contribute to group discussions
- Ask and answer questions based on what they have heard

They will also have non-verbal and visual information to take into account and need to identify what to ignore or filter out. No wonder school can be exhausting and confusing for those whose concentration and listening skills are weak.

The following pages highlight the characteristics of learners who have difficulties with listening and attentiveness, including those with weak working auditory memory and hearing impairment. Pages 31-40 look at ways to support and develop these pupils.

Attention!

It's easy to identify students with poor attention and limited ability to listen. Typically, they will:

1. Not look at who is speaking.
2. Lose motivation and 'switch off' if they know processing auditory information is difficult.
3. Be easily distracted by other auditory or visual information (eg a football match outside, your computer screensaver).
4. Daydream.
5. Not follow instructions.
6. Be unable to ask or answer relevant questions.
7. Lose track of group discussions.
8. Ask frequently for information to be repeated.
9. Say they don't understand or have forgotten.

> I have ADHD. I try to listen but then begin to daydream. In my head I go into another room and close the door. It's difficult when I come back to know what's going on.
> **Andrew, aged 11.**

Can you hear me?

Pupils with hearing impairment may also have difficulties with attention and listening. Over 80% of children with a hearing impairment are taught in mainstream schools. Many others will experience temporary deafness caused by ear infections, colds or build-up of ear wax. Any pupil with a history of hearing difficulties as a young child may not have developed adequate listening skills and may need to be taught these.

Indicators of possible hearing difficulties:
- Does not respond to name or instructions
- Relies on contextual clues, such as body language or lip reading
- Speaks too softly or too loudly
- Unable to eliminate background noise, eg buzzing projector or air conditioning
- Often asks for help or repetition
- Misses information that has been given
- Unable to discriminate between similar sounding words (eighteen/ eighty)
- Has difficulty with dictation and mental maths
- May appear uninterested, inattentive or 'in their own world'

I repeat, can you hear me?

Most children with permanent hearing loss are identified before they begin school. Depending on the severity of the loss some children will require little support in school; others may need intensive support throughout their education.

Pupils with hearing aids or cochlear implants need to sit near the front as hearing aids work best 1-2 metres away from the speaker. They also amplify background noise, so avoid seating positions next to blow heaters or buzzing machinery.

Hearing impaired pupils need lots of visual backup to follow class discussions. Small adjustments can make a big difference, eg displaying video subtitles, and avoiding walking around the room or standing in the shadows when you are speaking.

If you think a pupil's hearing has deteriorated or seems patchy, speak to their parents and your SENCO or school nurse. Middle-ear infections and glue ear are very common in young children and GPs can advise on treatment options.

Auditory memory

'*It goes in one ear and out the other.*' This statement is close to the truth for pupils with weak auditory memory. Think of working auditory memory as our brain's Post-it note for the words that we hear. It is the ability to hold on to information long enough to process and understand it.

Pupils make demands on their working memory constantly in the classroom: holding on to numbers when doing maths calculations, for example, or remembering the sequence of events when listening to a story. Working auditory memory also helps us to keep track of what has been said in a conversation and to remember what we still have to say. Many children with SLCN have a weak working auditory memory.

Jenny can only take in and remember three to four words at a time. After that she subconsciously stops listening so that she can process the words. She then starts to listen again. As the pattern continues it becomes increasingly confusing, boring and difficult for her to understand and maintain attention. Imagine it:

'Today we are going... VIII and his six... and beheaded another... survived...'

Ermmm... I've forgotten that already

Having a weak working auditory memory can have a significant impact on learning in the classroom. Pupils may:

- Easily forget instructions, especially those that are long and complex
- Raise their hand but forget what they wanted to say
- Miss out stages within an activity
- Carry out only the beginning or end of an instruction
- Lose track in conversations and discussions
- Be disorganised and forget equipment or homework
- Copy others all of the time
- Appear to be listening attentively but not be taking anything in
- Be unable to relay a message accurately
- Struggle with mental maths and oral discussion

So what classroom strategies and activities can support pupils in developing effective attention, listening and memory skills?

Mind your language!

The first thing you can do to is to check your own language and make adjustments where necessary:

- Set the scene by giving an overview first and then going into more detail
- Give pointers for what pupils should listen to. *'It is important that you remember X'*
- Use short sentences and bite-size chunks of language
- Speak slowly and insert more pauses than usual
- Repeat and rephrase to offer more opportunities to grasp what you are saying
- Check understanding regularly. Ask pupils to summarise what you have said
- Support your language with visual clues: gesture, objects, drawings, diagrams

If you speak with a strong regional accent pupils may need time to get used to this.

Teacher talk

Other tactics include:

> Ross, I'd like you to write your name at the top of the page.

- Using a pupil's name at the beginning of an instruction. It's a simple but powerful way of grabbing their attention
- Facing pupils when speaking and ensuring they are all facing you. Seeing your lips move, your facial expression and gestures all aid understanding and help pupils to stay focused
- Reducing background noise or distractions (A game of netball on the playground or music from a neighbouring classroom can be far more interesting to pupils than Pythagoras' theorem)
- Asking TAs to support your explanations non-verbally where possible. They could draw a picture or diagram of what you are explaining to boost pupils' understanding
- Using the 10-second rule. After asking a question, allow 10 seconds before expecting an answer. This gives pupils time to listen, to process what has been said, and to formulate their thoughts. It's a simple but effective support

Giving instructions

Following verbal instructions is challenging for students who have difficulties with memory, sequencing and organisation.

Instructions in **written or visual form** can support memory, as can a **physical demonstration** or **modelling**. Students are more likely to remember what equipment you said they would need for a science experiment if they have watched you get it out and set it up, and if they have a visual reminder to refer to as well.

Imagine the confusion this instruction caused for pupils who struggle with sequential concepts such as 'before' and 'after':

'After you have finished your posters I want you to write your homework in your diary and get your reading books out. But before that you need to tidy up. And don't forget to put your name on your work first.'

A more helpful version:

'**First** put your names on your posters and tidy up. **Next** we will write the homework in our diaries **and then** we will get our reading books out.'

Teaching active listening skills

We often tell pupils to 'listen carefully' without teaching them explicitly *how* to listen. Here are six active listening skills that pupils with SLCN may need to be taught:

1. Look at the speaker.
2. Sit still.
3. Ignore environmental distractions.
4. Think about the words you are hearing.
5. Consider body language and other non-verbal signs.
6. Ask for clarification when needed.

(Based on ideas from Active Listening for Active Learning. Johnson & Player, 2009)

Explain how looking and sitting still helps them to focus on the speaker and how thinking about what is said will help with making a relevant response. Use role plays to illustrate this.

Can you clarify that?

Teach pupils how to ask for clarification.

Display sentence starters to help them with this and build opportunities into lessons for them to ask you or their peers for help:

Not sure what to do?

- 'One word I didn't understand was...'
- 'Could you tell me what X means?'
- 'One thing I would like you to explain again is ...'
- 'Could you check I have understood this?'
- 'I think we have to ...... Have I left anything out?'

Practising listening

Many everyday classroom activities provide opportunities to reinforce attention and listening skills as well as subject content and can be adapted for all age groups.

1. Key words bingo. When watching video clips ask pupils to keep a tally of key vocabulary. Give them a list of words or icons on a bingo-style card to tick off. They can call 'bingo' when they have a line.

2. The fishbowl. Ask four pupils to sit in the centre of the room and discuss a previously taught topic. The rest of the class have to observe the 'fish' and feed back on how well they listened and communicated. Observers may be asked to comment on body language, eye contact, the relevance of questions and answers given, and appropriateness.

3. Speaker, listener, observer. Pupils work in groups of three. The speaker tells the listener about a topic covered in class. The listener then has to re-tell what the speaker has said. The observer comments on how much the listener remembered and whether anything was left out.

Show don't tell

Try the following ideas to add visual support for attention, listening and memory.

Get arty. Use stick drawings or cartoons to illustrate what you are talking about. Creating comic strips and storyboards is a simple and effective way of supporting memory, sequencing and understanding in eg, English, Humanities, Science.

Here's one I made earlier. Show finished examples of the work, task or experiment you are about to set up so that pupils can see what they have to achieve.

Make it real. Bring in objects from home or find pictures and video on the internet to accompany verbal explanation. Widgit software (see page 125) is a quick way of creating visual wordlists and task boards.

Get dramatic. Use gesture and body language to convey what you mean. Perform role plays or act out events. This grabs attention as well as making information more memorable.

Remember, remember

As adults we use a range of strategies to help us listen to and remember information. We take notes in meetings, store information on our phones, write notes to ourselves and make lists. Pupils with SLCN will need to be taught these strategies explicitly.

Use **modern technology**. If your pupils use tablets, laptops or smartphones, teach them how to make voice memos or use a 'notes' app or the 'sticky notes' accessory in Windows (the electronic version of a Post-it note).

Encourage pupils to note down **key information**, numbers or instructions on mini-whiteboards, in their books, or on Post-it notes. Older pupils can be taught how to make bullet-point lists, and use planning frames and **task boards**.

Task boards

Task boards present instructions visually. Like a recipe or flat-pack assembly guide, they show what to do, the order to do it in and how the finished product will look. With a task board 'reminder' pupils can work independently in class or at homework.

Can be filled in with words and/ or pictures

Can be filled in by the teacher, a TA, or the pupil

Supports pupils' ability to break down tasks into manageable steps

Aids organisation, memory and sequencing

Older pupils can fill in a task board as a way of checking they have understood and of helping them to plan and think through what they will do

Strategies to support working auditory memory

1. **Be calm and patient.** The memorisation process works best when the situation is stress-free so don't rush or draw attention to a pupil's difficulties.

2. **Verbalisation.** If we say something in our own voice, we are more likely to remember it. Encourage pupils to repeat information back to themselves and verbally rehearse what they want to say. As a practice technique, ask a pupil to deliver a verbal message to another member of staff. Messages that require a reply have a built-in check mechanism.

3. **Keep it simple.** Practise different, simple ways of remembering, eg counting the different steps in a task on your fingers or physically rehearsing something.

4. **Visualisation.** Many commercial memory resources and games support visual rather than auditory memory. However, visualisation can support working auditory memory. Encourage pupils to 'visualise' what they hear, providing icons or pictures if they find it difficult. The game *'I went to market and I bought... ...'* is a way of practising memory and visualisation. It's also useful for reinforcing subject-specific vocabulary. Limit how much there is to remember by playing in small groups at first.

Understanding Language

Receptive language difficulties

Paying attention and listening is just half the battle; we then have to process and understand what we have heard. Students who struggle to understand what is said to them, or what they read, have difficulties with **receptive language**. The message is transmitted, but may not be fully received.

Pupils with a **general learning difficulty** or developmental delay will have receptive language difficulties commensurate with their general level of development.

Those who have a **specific difficulty** with receptive language will fall within the average range for understanding and solving non-verbal tasks such as number or visual puzzles. However, their struggle to understand language is a huge barrier to learning in the classroom, where they are often expected to learn through listening or reading.

Difficulties with attention and listening and receptive language are closely linked. It's not easy to know if pupils don't understand because they aren't listening, or aren't listening because they don't understand.

What are you talking about?

'We were told we would be making mobiles. I was really excited about making a new phone but we made coat hangers that hang from the ceiling instead.' (Y9 pupil)

It's easy for pupils with SLCN to 'get the wrong end of the stick'. Typically, children with receptive language difficulties develop coping strategies that hide their language needs. You may notice that some pupils:

I find a lot of what the teachers say really boring. I don't know what they are going on about. (Lisa, aged 10)

- Avoid answering questions, or offer answers that miss the mark
- Try to control the conversation and talk to you about things they are sure of
- May use lots of learned or repeated phrases, eg 'anyway'
- Wait for others to start tasks so they can copy them and see what to do
- Find it hard to learn and retain new vocabulary
- Don't follow instructions even though they appeared to be listening attentively
- Frequently misunderstand or misinterpret situations

What I mean is…?

Again, when teaching students with receptive language difficulties start with your own language:

- Say what you mean. Explain words or phrases that have multiple meanings or contain figurative language. Idioms (*'pull your socks up'*), metaphors (*'are you an early bird or night owl?'*) and even single words with more than one meaning can cause confusion
- Give pupils plenty of time to think about what you have said. Check their understanding regularly
- Say what you want to happen rather than what you don't want to see. Positive statements are easier to follow:

 I want you to sit still and listen carefully.

 I don't want any monkey business or messing about. You know what happened last week and we don't want a repeat performance, do we?

But I understand perfectly

Often pupils with SLCN don't realise that they've not understood. Poor auditory discrimination skills mean that pupils sometimes 'mishear' words for ones they already know. They then build their learning around this.

> In a year 6 group discussion Lauren spoke at length about how she had learned to curtsey in ballet class at the weekend. Joel and Tommy both confirmed that they understood what Lauren had shared. Joel said his mum had been given 'loads of courtesy cars too' and that's what Lauren's mum must have. Tommy said his sister's best friend was called Kirsty and that's who Lauren must have met at the weekend.

Effective and frequent questions targeted specifically at checking understanding can help to clarify misunderstandings as can using plenty of visual back up. Create an environment in your classroom that encourages pupils to ask whenever they hear a new word or don't understand.

Linking the language to something else

People learn best when auditory information is supported by visual, tactile or experience-based learning. Children with SLCN find language so confusing that it is difficult to create a picture of it in their heads. They hear something and then it is gone.

Reinforcing visuals can help to 'fix' the language and allow pupils to 'hold' it long enough to process and make sense of it. Whether on a white board, task board (see page 39), poster, number line, visual dictionary or glossary, accessible visual aids keep learners on task and promote independence.

Similarly, if you can link new information to something a pupil already knows, this acts as a hook on which to attach the new idea:

- Teaching 'friction' in Science? Take your class to the playground slide

- Teaching 'ratio' in Maths? Bring in some orange squash. One part squash to five parts water tastes very different from five parts squash and one part water

Understanding concepts

Sometimes it is not just a word or sentence that causes confusion, but the concept itself. **Concepts** are abstract ideas whose meaning can be hard to define. Compared with words that name items or describe actions, words that denote ideas, emotions, feelings, or qualities are tricky to grasp. Think about how difficult it is to define these concepts in just one or two words:

PEACE   **EVAPORATION**   **TIME**   **KNOWLEDGE**

Furthermore, some concepts are relative: they change their meaning depending on time or the perspective of the speaker. Take *'left and right'* (the speaker's left could be your right); *'a long time'* (30 minutes, 3 hours, 300 years?); *'soon'* (now, 5 minutes, 30 minutes, next week, next month?). It's confusing.

Similarly, be aware of words with more than one meaning:

Peace vs Noise   **Peace vs War**

Teaching concepts

Concepts are easier to grasp when we learn about them in a variety of ways.

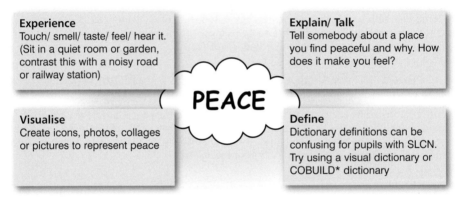

Experience
Touch/ smell/ taste/ feel/ hear it.
(Sit in a quiet room or garden,
contrast this with a noisy road
or railway station)

Explain/ Talk
Tell somebody about a place
you find peaceful and why. How
does it make you feel?

PEACE

Visualise
Create icons, photos, collages
or pictures to represent peace

Define
Dictionary definitions can be
confusing for pupils with SLCN.
Try using a visual dictionary or
COBUILD* dictionary

*The Collins COBUILD dictionary was created for people with English as a second language.
It gives easy-to-understand definitions, using simple vocabulary and examples. It is available
in hard copy or at www.collinsdictionary.com*

Other difficulties with concepts

Time concepts (eg remembering the sequence of days or months, or distinguishing between lengths of time) pose problems for pupils with SLCN. *'You have five more minutes on this task'* can be meaningless. A visual timer on your whiteboard will help pupils 'see' how much time is left. Try *www.online-stopwatch.com/classroom-timers/*

Timelines of events, flow charts and visual timetables (with symbols/pictures to show what is happening and in which order) are useful resources across the age range.

Number concepts pose similar problems. Number lines (especially for negative numbers), and visuals to explain fractions, decimals and percentages are invaluable. Classroom resources such as plastic money, cuisenaire rods and Base 10 sets can reinforce place value, addition, subtraction, multiplication and division concepts.

What isn't said

Inference is the ability to understand what isn't explicit in text or speech and many pupils with language difficulties find it hard to pick up on implied information.

Consider some of the instructions that pupils come across:

> Homework needs to be completed by Wednesday.

You might think you've been clear but not all pupils will infer from this that they have to bring the homework to the lesson or hand it in by Wednesday, regardless of whether or not they have a lesson that day.

> It's getting very noisy in here. I can't hear myself think.

If you imply rather than state explicitly that pupils need to be quiet, some students won't pick up on your intended meaning.

Inference in films, plays and books

Do your pupils talk eagerly about a film or drama they've seen, but then seem to have missed the whole point of the plot? It could be that they haven't understood the hidden story. Many pupils find the demands of inference in narrative beyond them. The following strategies work with whole classes. For younger children you can provide the support materials; older students can make their own:

- Make sure pupils know and can name all the characters in a book or film. Draw them (or find pictures to represent them) and, as a class, talk about the kind of people they are
- Make a 'people map' or family tree to show how the characters are related to each other. Add to it as new characters are introduced
- Use drama to explore character and narrative. Role play, hotseating and acting out key moments, can all help pupils to understand characters' motives
- Make comic strips and storyboards, or use commercially available comics to show narrative sequence and development
- Chunk the plot into smaller sub-plots, perhaps creating a timeline for each character or location

Using language to reason and problem solve

Problem solving tasks can be frustrating for pupils with language weaknesses, particularly in Maths and Science for students who are confident with number and numeric processes but do badly in tests because of the language involved. Problem solving requires the ability to isolate the key information and to manipulate information in a reasoned and logical way.

Pupils need to be able to:

- Identify the key information
- Break the problem down into stages
- Remember each stage of a task to carry it on to the next stage
- Recognise when they've got the finishing information

Keep questions on tests and exams as clear and easy to understand as possible.

'Put these numbers in order from smallest to biggest – 99, 19, 8, 45, 76'. *'But they all look the same size to me! Do I need to measure them with a ruler?'*

How do you solve a problem?

Ben is presented with the following problem:

I go out to meet a friend in town and I buy a coffee for £1.50 and a piece of chocolate cake for £1. How much change will I get if I pay with a £5 note?

If presented with the calculations £1.50 + £1 and £5.00 – £2.50 he could produce the right answer but he can't solve this problem because of the language it's 'wrapped up in'.

1. Ask Ben to highlight the key words (the numbers and words that tell you what to do).
2. Help him to identify the kind of answer that it will be (ie an amount of money).
3. Use a problem-solving sheet to help him keep a visual track of the stages. Or, draw simple pictures and stick people to show what is happening.

Showing Ben how to take notes and show his working out as he goes along helps him to keep track of what he is doing.

Understanding written text

Many pupils struggle to make sense of text even when they can read the words. They may even be able to say what all the individual words mean but have limited comprehension of the whole.

Don't assume that watching 'the film of the book' will help. A film may hold their attention and they will remember some key scenes but, as we saw earlier, the story will often move too fast for them to keep up and they may still have problems picking up inferences.

Help pupils keep track of a longer story by providing a blank wipe-clean bookmark or folded piece of paper for inside their book. At the end of each chapter pupils think about what has happened, note key information and names or draw quick pictures to jog their memory ready for the next time they come to the story.

Pronouns

Pronouns can be particularly confusing for some pupils when reading. Not all children automatically know that they have to look back over what they have already read to find out what, say, *'he'*, *'she'*, *'it'* or *'they'* refers to. Colour coding or highlighting works well. Take the following example:

Bill found a dog in the park when he was out jogging on Wednesday morning. It was dirty and scrawny.

If asked what the dog was like, some pupils will say they don't know. They look back to the word 'dog' in the first sentence and aren't any better informed. They need to work out what 'it' represents at the beginning of the second sentence. Trying out the various possibilities will reveal which option makes sense.

The park was dirty and scrawny

Wednesday morning was dirty and scrawny

The dog was dirty and scrawny

Look who's talking

In texts which contain several lines of dialogue it can be tricky to work out which character is speaking. Again, highlighters or colour coding work well to help identify who is talking. Alternatively, depending on the age of your students:

- Make stickers for key characters in the text to affix next to their contributions
- Use speech-bubble-shaped Post-it notes to help pupils put dialogue into their own words which they then attach to pictures of characters
- Make stick puppets of figures and speak the text. This will also help pupils remember who is in a story and recognise inferences

Speech

Spotting speech difficulties

It's now time to look at language **output**, ie how we *use* language, rather than how we receive and understand it.

A difficulty with speech is one of the easiest types of SLCN to spot but it can be hard to know what to do to help, especially with older pupils, who may be acutely embarrassed about their difficulties. Pupils with this category of SLCN may:

- Be consistently unclear or mumble when talking
- Avoid talking or reading aloud
- Talk with a hand in front of their mouth or so quietly that it is impossible to hear
- Not contribute in lessons or class discussion
- Get another pupil to talk on their behalf
- Be absent on days when oral presentations or class assemblies are scheduled

When is a problem not a problem?

Speech difficulties are more common in primary aged children. Most children will be able to say most sounds by the time they are around 5 years old. Some sounds, though, are particularly difficult. It's not unusual for 6- or 7-year-olds to still struggle with 'l' 'r' and 'th'. This isn't something to worry about, especially if literacy skills are developing well and you can usually understand what is said.

This section looks in turn at each of the three main areas of speech difficulty you are likely to encounter and then considers support strategies.

Types of speech difficulty

1. **Stammering/ stuttering** – the repetition of words or parts of words and hesitant, staccato speaking.

2. **Speech sound difficulties**
   a) **Phonological difficulties** (see page 65) – pupils use incorrect sounds when they speak (eg a 't' sound instead of a 'c/k' sound). This is common in younger children but can persist in some children until they are much older. When talking, they will sound like much younger children and may have associated spelling and literacy difficulties, even when their speech problems are no longer evident.

   b) **Articulation** – includes pupils who have:
   - A single sound difficulty such as a 'lisp' or shushy 's' sound.
   - Problems forming sounds accurately as a result of motor difficulties such as dyspraxia or cerebral palsy

   Tat!

3. **Voice disorders** – voice difficulties, such as a persistently hoarse or breathy, quiet voice which is not associated with a cold or throat infection.

Stammering, stuttering or dysfluency?

Stuttering and **stammering** are different names for the same difficulty. Any persistent disruption in the fluency of talking is technically called a **dysfluency**. For the purposes of this book, we will use the term 'stammer'.

Stammering includes:
- Repeating sounds, words, or parts of words
- Abnormally long pauses with a struggle to talk usually at the start of a phrase or sentence
- Unusual facial or body movements that accompany the speech

> My stammer gets worse when I am upset or excited. I need people to be extra patient when they are listening to me.
> Dan, aged 14

There is no known cause of stammering, although it can run in families. There is also no cure, although many people, with support and therapy, develop good control of their stammers. We do know that good supportive management at school and home can help a pupil become more fluent.

Many young children stammer as part of their development but most will not go on to stammer as teenagers and adults.

How can I help a pupil who stammers?

Stammerers sometimes develop 'tricks' to help them get their words out, such as tapping their fingers or stamping a foot. Although these tricks seem helpful at first, they often become less effective over time and, at worst, become part of the problem: the person now not only sounds different but behaves differently too.

A stammer usually needs expert help* so never be afraid to suggest a referral to speech and language therapy services. There are, though, some simple strategies you and other pupils in the class can use to support a student who stammers:

- Allow time for the pupil to answer. Being rushed or feeling that someone is going to take your turn will increase the stammer
- Keep calm. Try not to show your own anxiety, concern and embarrassment
- Use a slower rate of speech yourself. Slowing down your own rate of talking will automatically help your pupil speak more slowly and fluently
- Be aware that having to speak in front of others, or on the phone, or when emotions are running high raises the stakes and makes a stammer worse

*See the British Stammering Association www.stammering.org for information and resources.

More ways to support

It can often be a real relief for anyone who stammers to talk about their difficulties:

- Find a quiet time, away from other pupils, and acknowledge the difficulty, *'I've noticed that sometimes you get stuck with your talking'*

- Plan ahead for tricky situations (oral exams, presentations, assemblies). Ask the pupil how you can help to make the situation less threatening, eg making a recording or video to show instead of standing in front of the class might reduce nerves and anxiety

- Reading or speaking with someone else in unison often makes a pupil more fluent and increases confidence. Teachers report that when a pupil sings or speaks in unison their stammer disappears. The same thing can happen when talking with background music playing through headphones. It's not always clear why these things work; it may be the rhythm of the music that helps, or not being able to hear themselves speak

Speech sound difficulties

Speech sound difficulties are among the commonest kinds of SLCN, especially in Early Years and KS1. The following will help **all** children with unclear speech sounds and will help you interact more confidently with them:

- Be a good model: speak slowly and clearly yourself
- Try to face the child when you are talking so that they can see the sounds as well as hear what you are saying
- If you haven't understood what a child says ask them to show you in writing or drawing. Or tell them what you have understood and which parts you need help with. *'OK, I know that you are telling me about the football and the window, but I didn't get the bit in the middle. Can you tell me about that in another way, please?'* This gives the child some positive feedback and guidance about which words they need to work on
- Don't just ask the child to repeat a word they can't say over and over again. Do model the correct word clearly in your follow up sentence so that the child can hear accurate sounds
- Don't assume laziness – many sounds are harder to say in some words than others

What are phonological difficulties?

Phonology is the study of the sound system in language. Phonological difficulties are difficulties with how we recognise, discriminate, say and add meaning to the different sounds of language.

Phonological speech difficulties are relatively common in pre-school children, but by the time most children enter school, although their speech sounds may not be perfect, they should be intelligible most of the time.

A pupil with phonological **delay** will sound like a much younger child. A 5-year-old may say 'bish' instead of 'fish'; in a 2-year-old this wouldn't be unexpected. Children with a phonological **disorder** will mix up or mispronounce words in an unusual or unexpected way and are much harder to understand.

Basic phonological awareness underpins later literacy skills. Typically developing children play with sounds from a very early age and easily acquire phonic knowledge and literacy. Others – some later diagnosed with dyslexia, hearing impairment, or who have had limited exposure to speech at home – may not acquire these skills so easily. Often, though, there is no known cause for phonological difficulties.

Recognising phonological difficulties

Pupils with phonological difficulties tend to struggle to learn new and complex words. Pronunciation, segmenting words into syllables, recognising rhyme and speaking also pose problems.

Why is phonological awareness important? We need to work out the sound structure of an unknown word before we can begin to learn, retain and recall it, eg:

Jabberwocky

Starts with a 'j' sound
4 syllables (**jabb-er-wock-y**)
Ends with an 'ee' sound
8 sounds (**j-a-bb-er-w-o-ck-y**)
11 letters

In English the way we write sounds doesn't always correspond to the number of sounds we say. The sound 'sh' is represented by 2 letters but is just one sound; the word *'car'* has 2 spoken sounds: [c] and [ah], but we write 3 letters. Pupils find this confusing, especially when it comes to sounding out words. Poor phonological awareness affects reading and spelling skills.

Phonological awareness skills

There are four basic stages of phonological awareness* and many easy-to-prepare classroom activities to develop these skill sets. It's important to develop a pupil's listening and discrimination skills before they can change their speech sounds.

1. **Awareness that a spoken sentence consists of separate words**
   - Sing action songs (eg *Head, Shoulders, Knees and Toes...*) and nursery rhymes
   - Make an action when you hear a certain word in a story
   - Count the words in a spoken sentence
   - Who can create the longest sentence? Can anybody add one more word, or two words?

2. **Awareness that words are made up of syllables**
   - 'Collect' long words and clap out or jump for each syllable as you say the word. You can do the same with football team names or names of celebrities
   - Start all pupils at one side of the room. They take it in turns to say a topic word, the longest they can think of, and take one step forward for each syllable in the word. The winner is the first to the other side

* Based on *Developing Phonological Awareness Skills for Struggling Readers*. **R. Eachus, 2011**

Phonological awareness skills

3. **Awareness that syllables are made up of separate sounds**
   - Find the 'odd one out'. Which word doesn't rhyme? (eg *cat, hat, hug, mat*)
   - Play rhyming bingo (call out *'sing'*, pupils can mark off *'ring'*). This can be done with pictures instead of words to encourage pupils to 'hear' the rhyme rather than see similar letters written down
   - Who can find the most words that rhyme with …?

4. **Awareness that sounds can be manipulated within words**
   - Find words that begin or end with the same sound
   - Make alliterations (*'I am Calum the crazy crocodile'*)

Some pupils will need to revisit these skills. Computer intervention programmes such as 'Lexion' (aged 6-16) and 'Phoneme Factory' target phonological awareness skills. A growing number of apps for tablets and smartphones target auditory discrimination skills, sound matching, sound sequencing and phonic knowledge. Ask your school's speech and language therapist or learning support team which would be most suitable for individual pupils.

Articulation

Articulation difficulties occur when a child speaks unclearly because of a physical difficulty, eg:

- Low muscle tone
- Physical disabilities such as cerebral palsy
- Cranio-facial abnormalities such as cleft lip and palate
- Motor organisation and coordination difficulties

Pupils with speech difficulties of this type are most likely to have 'shushy' or unusual sounds in their talking. They may also dribble or have difficulty eating.

Many of the strategies offered already in this chapter are valid for pupils with articulation difficulties. Bear in mind that if a pupil is tired, upset, carrying out another motor activity (eg writing or walking) or is physically uncomfortable, talking will be harder.

Phonological and articulation difficulties – what can I do?

1. Give opportunities to hear new and complex words in isolation and more than once.

2. Talk through the sound structure of the word. Clap out the number of syllables and ensure pupils can say each sound. Talk about the first and last sounds of the word. Which other words begin with the same sound? Can the pupil generate any rhymes? Give pupils a chance to practise and then check they are saying the word correctly.

3. Offer a variety of ways for pupils to contribute to a discussion:
   - Writing and reading out a word on a mind map is less threatening than just saying a word. It also helps others know what has been said if speech is unclear
   - Ask pupils to label or talk about a diagram or other visual stimulus so that you can see what they are referring to
   - Computer programs such as WriteOnline and Writing In Symbols, as well as the 'Narrator' function in Microsoft Office, can read aloud what pupils have typed. Pupils can hear what they've written and check they've chosen the correct words

What are voice disorders?

Our voices are made in the larynx, or 'voice box'. Two flaps of skin called vocal cords come together and vibrate the air that we breathe out from our lungs between them.

Not all speech uses a voice. Some consonant sounds such as 'p' and 's' are whispered or quiet sounds and don't use our voice at all.

Try this: rest two fingers lightly on the front of your neck – about midway down on the Adam's apple. Now say a long 'sssssssssssss' sound. Keep your fingers in the same place and say a long 'zzzzzzzzzzzzzz' sound. You should be able to feel your vocal cords vibrating in the larynx and making the voice for the 'z' but not the 's' sound.

Voice problems occur when the vocal cords can't come together and vibrate properly. As a result, the voice may be hoarse and croaky, breathy and quiet, tight and squeaky, or a mixture of all these.

Supporting pupils with voice disorders

In young people, voice disorders often occur because of vocal abuse, particularly shouting, screaming or talking at high volume. Appropriate treatment of a voice disorder avoids damage to the vocal cords and restores a normal voice. Maintaining good voice use will prevent recurrence of the disorder.

- Encourage pupils to use the minimum volume they need to be heard
- Avoid asking a pupil to talk over a distance, (eg across a field or hall) or over background noise. In a science lab or computer room where pupils may need to raise their voices to be heard, ask them to come to you to talk, or you go to them
- Allow regular drinks – small sips of water are best for keeping the throat hydrated
- Discourage the pupil from coughing excessively or clearing their throat – a sip of water is better

 Looking after your own voice is just as important as looking after your pupils' voices. The *Vocal Skills Pocketbook* provides advice and information on this.

Using Language

What are expressive language difficulties?

This section of the Pocketbook looks at the way we use language to express ourselves. Students with **expressive language** difficulties may struggle to find the right word to label items or may struggle to structure their sentences and accounts, in both speech and writing. They may also find it difficult to explain their reasoning and thinking. Word finding difficulties will be covered later under 'Vocabulary', so this section focuses on:

- Sentences (word order and sentence construction)
- Structuring longer narrative and accounts

Pupils with general learning difficulties or developmental delay will have expressive language difficulties in line with their general level of development, but other pupils may have a specific difficulty with expressive language: they will have an average understanding of language but be unable to express what they know effectively. This latter group can become disheartened and disengaged very quickly. However hard they work they can't seem to get it right or show what they know. This can have a negative effect on self-esteem as well as earning them a reputation of being 'lazy' or not trying hard enough.

Familiar?

If any of your pupils sound or write like this they can be said to have difficulties with expressive language:

> Err the man ... er Roman ... err Romeo, I mean, he, well he and mates are going to... er the place, you know, like where this party is.. and there's a big argument.

> Yesterday I wented to fair and goed on dodgems and had candy floss and Sam comed too

> my dog got puppies they is called meg bob Dan when they eat mum give him special milk and dog food

Expressive language difficulties in the classroom

The following characteristics are typical of students with expressive language difficulties:

- Rarely contribute to small group or class discussion
- Talk in very short, 'immature' sentences
- Start to say something, but trail off and let others finish
- Can talk in long rambling sentences that are difficult to follow. Their writing may be like this too
- Use grammatical rules incorrectly and out of step with their age, taking into account their local accent and dialect
- Written work is poorly structured and lacks punctuation
- Homework that requires a high level of reading or writing is often incomplete and has too many pictures to the amount of text
- Text is copied word for word from another source of information

When sentences go wrong

Once we know the words we want to use, we have to put them together into sentences. Constructing sentences that convey what we intend them to can be trickier than we think. So, how can sentence building go wrong?

Word order. *'My sister not was there yesterday.'*

'Little words'. Using pronouns and possessive pronouns (he, they, hers, its) can cause confusion and lead to misunderstandings. *'Tom and Jack had a fight and Tom banged his head against the wall.'* (Whose head? Jack's or his own?)

Morphology. This is the way we change words to add meaning, eg by adding –*ing* or –*ed* to verbs to change the tense. *'She catched the ball and throwed it and we win.'*

Complex sentences and using connectives. Difficulties with negatives, connectives, conjunctions and longer sentences can make it difficult to understand what a pupil is trying to say: *'I will answer the question unless I put my hand up'*.

What do words do?

To construct a sentence we have to know the functions of words, not just what they mean.

In English a simple sentence usually starts with a *noun* (driver) and an *article* (the) to which we then add a *verb* (racing):
The driver was racing.

To add more information we can insert a *preposition* (along) and a location.
The driver was racing along the motorway.

Adjectives (tired, wet) give more information about the nouns.
The tired driver was racing along the wet motorway.

Adding an *adverb* (recklessly) can tell us how he was driving.
The tired driver was racing recklessly along the wet motorway.

A *conjunction* (and) allows us to join another clause
The tired driver was racing recklessly along the wet motorway and listening to an ABBA CD.

Pronouns (he, it) allow us to avoid repetition:
He changed it in favour of something more soothing.

Putting words in the right order

Some pupils will benefit from being taught parts of speech and how sentences are put together. Posters or word mats that classify words into their grammatical functions can be useful resources for pupils to refer to when speaking or writing.

You can also easily build sentence construction games into lessons. Start with a simple sentence and see if pupils can add in one element at a time – an adjective, an adverb, a prepositional phrase, a conjunction. Beginning with a sentence related to the current topic can also help to revise content (eg *Romeo went to a party… …; The volcano erupted… …*).

Alternatively, give students a 'type of word' card each (noun, verb, adjective, etc). Pupils stand in a line to create a sentence and may only contribute a word that is their part of speech. As pupils are called out they have to find the right place in the line for their word.

Ask for help. If a pupil consistently uses incorrect word order they will often need a speech and language therapy assessment to unravel the patterns in their sentences.

Morphology

Pupils with a history of speech sound difficulties or dyslexia may struggle to make the small changes to words that give extra information. In English these changes usually indicate plurals, possession or a different tense.

When teaching new words in your subject, try to introduce all their variants. If your pupils have vocabulary books, a word wall or exercise books, make sure they record the plural as well as singular form of nouns, eg fox/ foxes; goose/ geese; person/ people; sheep/ sheep.

When introducing new verbs teach all the verb endings. Ask pupils to complete sentences which require them to use the various forms:

- At the moment the volcano *is erupting*
- The volcano might *erupt* next week
- The volcano *was erupting* while people were running from their homes
- Last week the volcano *erupted*
- The volcano *erupts* every 80 years or so

Conjunctions

Conjunctions **connect** words, phrases, clauses or sentences. Difficulties in constructing complex sentences arise when pupils don't understand what different conjunctions mean.

Some common conjunctions

and   or   although

but   as   since

yet   before

if

because   after

while   when

both...and   unless

neither... nor

Practising conjunctions

- **Heads and Tails** – see if pupils can match beginnings and ends of sentences
- **Cloze exercises** – pupils fill in missing conjunctions
- **Finish the sentence** (orally or written) – *'It is important to wear goggles in the lab when....'; 'You should hang up coats in the lab because ...'; 'Tell your teacher immediately if...'*
- **Use in writing** – provide reminders (and examples) of conjunctions you would like pupils to use in their writing before they begin

Narrative – a story and a life skill

The ability to put ideas together in a coherent sequence that explains or expresses our thoughts and feelings requires all the word and sentence-level skills already mentioned in this book. Constructing extended oral or written narrative in this way is key to academic success and to creating a sense of self. To support learners with expressive language difficulties:

- **Start with the ideas**. Use mind maps, comic-style story boards, icons, key words or real objects to help pupils record and remember their ideas
- **Organise the ideas**. Using a method that enables students to physically move ideas around is great for helping them structure their thoughts. Mini whiteboards, computers and Post-it notes can be really helpful. Inspiration and WriteOnline (see page 125) both have mind-mapping tools which allow ideas to be moved around the screen. Many pupils benefit from rehearsing their answer with a TA or partner before writing or speaking to the class
- **Provide back up**. Pupils with SLCN often have trouble remembering what they have learnt, so provide a concrete, visual reminder of information they can talk or write about

Helping to build a narrative or account

As well as being a weak writer, Selina struggled to generate ideas and plan her stories. Often she would end up with just a couple of sentences that weren't linked and didn't make sense.

Her teacher suggested she worked with the TA to create a story using plastic figures and other objects. Selina moved these around to create a story and 'acted it out' with the figures. She talked it through with the assistant several times who then filmed the story on the iPad.

Selina then added an oral narrative which she could listen back to and improve. To help her literacy, she next moved on to making 'photo stories' with the figures and other objects, adding speech bubbles to characters and then captions. In this way Selina was able to build up and practise more complex narratives without being limited by her literacy levels.

Getting it onto paper

You can also support the writing process by providing:

1. Lists of keywords supported by symbols or pictures.
2. Writing frames and sentence starters to help pupils structure an account, eg:
   Should homework be banned at our school?
   Some people think that homework should be banned because …
   Other people would argue that…   In my opinion ….   In conclusion….
3. Dictionaries, thesauruses, electronic spellcheckers or voice-text software. 'Dragon' software, or Microsoft Office's speech recognition tool are useful for those who can express themselves well in speech but not in writing.
4. Feedback from adults or peers during the writing process, not only at the end.

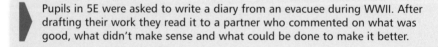

Pupils in 5E were asked to write a diary from an evacuee during WWII. After drafting their work they read it to a partner who commented on what was good, what didn't make sense and what could be done to make it better.

Vocabulary

What's in a word?

Vocabulary covers the words we use, their meanings and associations. This goes beyond the dictionary definition to include all the wider connotations of a word created by our personal experiences and the contexts in which we know it.

It is through vocabulary that we store and learn new concepts and ideas. We are all learning new vocabulary all the time. In recent years we have effortlessly processed and added to our lexicon words and phrases such as 'social media', 'selfie' and 'onesie'.

How pupils organise their vocabulary and link information affects their ability to use those words accurately and appropriately in speech and writing.

How do we learn new words?

Any word we don't recognise is a new word, whether it's real, invented, English or foreign. When children first hear a new word they need to work out what it means.

- They start to decipher the **sound structure**. First and last sounds? How many syllables?
- They may have the **written word** or a symbol or object to help them work out meaning
- **Interacting** with others can help them make sense of the new word
- They use the **context** and information around them to help. What would make sense?
- They consult their **inner lexicon** (their internal word store) and compare this word with others in their long term memory, trying to match it with similar sounding words

For the new word to become part of everyday language it will need to be used in self-generated talk and in different settings. Pupils also need to learn its various forms, eg its plural or different tenses.

Sound familiar?

Pupils with SLCN may struggle with several aspects of this vocabulary learning process, eg

1. Inventing a word because the 'correct' one isn't known.

> I walked through the field, Miss, and there was this huge cow family.

> We need to get out the telescope..no the er binoculars...no no the eye scope.

2. Muddling words/ not being able to find the right one.

3. Remembering the correct word but not its meaning.

> I know about *this, it's* precipitation isn't it? It's a *Geography* word. It means...er....errmmm.. something to do with Geography.

What are vocabulary difficulties?

Difficulties with learning vocabulary fall into a number of categories.

1. Some children can't identify the **sound structure** of the word. Without this information it is impossible to remember or learn it. (Revisit the 'Speech' chapter for advice).Think back to a time when you were introduced to somebody with an unfamiliar or 'foreign' name. How many times did you have to ask them to say their name before you could say it? Can you remember it now?

2. Other pupils may struggle to **recall** the word they want. They might use a generic term such as *'thingy'*, *'them'* or *'that one'*. They may say the opposite of the word they want or use a word that sounds similar (eg *'comic'* for *'comet'*). They might get round the problem imaginatively by describing the object or inventing a whole new term, eg a *'cup plate'* for *'saucer'*.

Which category?

3. Another potential stumbling block to building vocabulary is **organising**
   how to store words. Students with SLCN can find it hard to link words by
   meaning or to **categorise** them into groups or hierarchies.

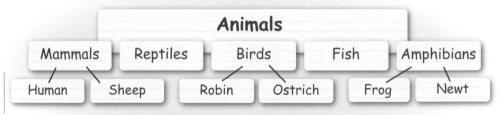

The next few pages look at specific strategies for supporting each of the types of difficulty
we've identified:

- **Sound structure**   • **Word retrieval**   • **Organisation and categorisation**

We'll then suggest broader, general strategies to help pupils develop and improve their
vocabulary learning.

Sound structure strategies

As we saw in the 'Speech' section, to learn the sound structure of a new word
we need to be able to segment it into syllables and sounds. This is why pupils with
limited phonological awareness struggle to learn, say and retain new vocabulary.

If you can unravel sound structure, you can sometimes add meaning.
Take the noun 'microscope' (mi/cro/scope) as an example:

micro = small   scope = looking ▷ a thing used for looking at small things

What helps?
- Saying the word slowly several times
- Tapping out syllables helps even older
  pupils to count them
- Practising each syllable separately then
  building the word syllable by syllable
- Looking at the spelling helps some
  learners but confuses those who struggle
  with sound-symbol correspondence
- Teaching meanings for prefixes and suffixes

Pass the thingamajig

We all know what it is like to experience word retrieval problems from time to time:

Pass me the ….
Oh…. the thing-a-ma-jig.

I met …. You know …. Your friend…What's his name? Oh…. It's on the tip of my tongue.

In pupils with SLCN, **word finding difficulties** are strongly related to problems with vocabulary learning and retention as well as with phonological awareness. Word finding difficulties can significantly impede verbal and written communication. If every sentence contains one or two words they are unable to retrieve quickly enough, it is frustrating for both speaker and audience.

Word retrieval strategies

To help a pupil who has trouble bringing to mind the word they want:

- Allow time for them to answer. Being rushed or feeling that someone is going to take your turn increases anxiety and makes it harder to retrieve the right word

- Try not to supply the elusive word yourself nor to let other pupils 'jump in' with it, before your student has had sufficient time to think

- Encourage the pupil to talk about the 'thing' whose name they are searching for:
  Pupil: *It's a ... oh erm ... erm...ermmm....*
  You: *What is it for? What do we do with it?*
  Pupil: *It's for plants, for watering... watering can!*

- Supply visual dictionaries and word lists; the picture can help them to find the word

- Use semantically organised rather than alphabetical word lists and dictionaries. If a student can't remember a word, they're unlikely to remember how it starts

Organising and categorising strategies

To help pupils store new words in the right category, show them the 'network' the word belongs to. Which category or family does it belong to? Which words mean the same or the opposite? Mind maps or spider diagrams are useful for this. A well organised lexicon with good associations for words helps retention and recall.

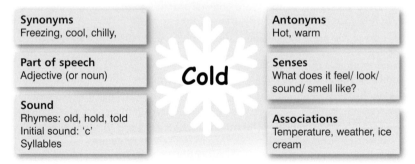

Synonyms
Freezing, cool, chilly,

Part of speech
Adjective (or noun)

Sound
Rhymes: old, hold, told
Initial sound: 'c'
Syllables

Cold

Antonyms
Hot, warm

Senses
What does it feel/ look/
sound/ smell like?

Associations
Temperature, weather, ice
cream

Odd one out – This quick game encourages students to think about categorising words and to explain associations. Supply four words, eg banana, apple, chair, cherry. Which is the odd one and why?

General strategies

It's not unusual for students to come across as many as 50 new words in the course of a week. How can you help them learn, and remember new vocabulary?

- Introduce new vocabulary in multiple ways (say it, use pictures and diagrams, write it, experience it). Repeat frequently; give examples of the word in context

- Wherever possible link a new word to a visual. This might be a diagram, photo, object or action. Pupils can make a visual word list or keep a vocabulary book

- Check that learners have secured the meaning of new words by asking them to describe or explain in their own words. A fun way to do this is by playing '**Taboo**'.

How to play Taboo
Make a set of cards displaying key words from the recent topic or unit of work. Pupils play in teams of two or more. A member of the first team picks a card and has to explain the word on it to the rest of the team, *without saying the key word*. Once somebody guesses correctly, the player takes another card and moves on to defining the next word. The team is awarded a point for each correct answer. After two minutes are up the next team then takes a turn. The team which guesses most words correctly wins!

False friends and infrequent visitors

1. Some words have more than one meaning. This can cause confusion, eg:

Table
- a piece of furniture
- **but in Science**
- columns of figures

Bank
- a place that looks after money
- **but in Geography**
- the side of a river

Mean
- nasty
- **but in Maths**
- average

When teaching subject specific vocabulary, ask pupils to tell you the everyday meaning first. Then teach the subject-specific meaning.

2. Think about some of the words you have introduced today that students are unlikely to hear or use outside your classroom, eg:

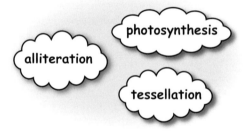

alliteration

photosynthesis

tessellation

Build in frequent opportunities for revisiting previously-taught vocabulary. Create a 'word wall' onto which you add new vocabulary, with pictures, for pupils to refer to.

Words, words everywhere

Having a wide vocabulary improves the ability to communicate effectively in a range of situations, both at school and socially. It also facilitates reading, listening and understanding and enables pupils to express themselves more precisely. Many pupils with SLCN have a smaller vocabulary than their peers. It is worth making vocabulary learning an integral part of school life.

- Encourage pupils to list new words that they read or hear, in school, at home or on television

- Teach and model ways of discovering the meaning of new words. Can they work it out from the context? Ask a friend or adult? Use a glossary or COBUILD dictionary?

- Use a thesaurus. Build in opportunities for redrafting writing using different words. Create games and activities that develop dictionary and thesaurus skills

Games to practise vocabulary

Vocabulary Bingo. Pupils write topic words on their 'bingo cards'. Instead of calling the words, call the definitions. Or vice versa - definitions on cards and call the words.

Sit Down When...' Begin with everyone standing. Give an instruction, eg *'Everybody sit down when I name a mammal'*. Those who don't sit down are 'out'.

Adverb Charades. A student acts out an activity (ironing, sawing, painting) and the class guess the manner (adverb) the pupil is acting (slowly, angrily, happily, etc).

Matching Pairs. Match definitions with words. This can be done with cards (like dominoes), on an interactive whiteboard or as a whole class activity – give out words and definitions, one to each pupil. Can they find their 'partner'?

Social Communication

What is social communication?

Having looked at how we use and understand language, it's time to consider the 'bigger picture'. **Social communication** is how we use and understand language in a range of social situations.

We continue to learn social communication skills through secondary school and beyond. Most teachers are easily able to identify pupils in their classes who need support with social skills: they're the students who seem to be inappropriate, rude or irritating; alternatively they may be shy and withdrawn.

This section of the book identifies the skills that make up social communication and offers strategies for helping pupils to develop them.

What are social communication skills?

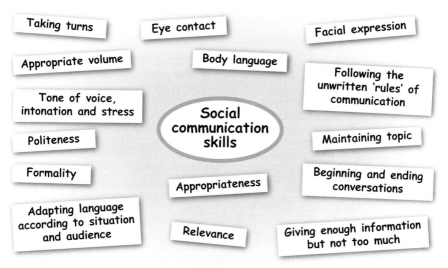

Taking turns

Eye contact

Facial expression

Appropriate volume

Body language

Following the unwritten 'rules' of communication

Tone of voice, intonation and stress

Social communication skills

Politeness

Maintaining topic

Formality

Beginning and ending conversations

Appropriateness

Adapting language according to situation and audience

Relevance

Giving enough information but not too much

Who has social communication difficulties?

All students with language difficulties will have secondary difficulties with social communication.

Hannah has Asperger syndrome. She struggles to know when it is her chance to talk in group discussion. She has difficulty maintaining conversations with peers but can talk for hours about her passion, video games.

Ro has a lot of friends and gets on well with them. He uses the same informal speech register with adults and people in authority as he does with his friends – slang, swearing, jokes, etc.

Quiet and withdrawn, Sunita never initiates conversations. She gives one-word answers when spoken to, whispering and looking at the floor.

Matt is confident and loves to talk. He often interrupts and talks over others, jumping from one subject to the next. It can be difficult to know what he is talking about and he doesn't take into account other people's responses.

Get yourselves into groups...

Students with weak social communication skills find group work and peer assessment particularly challenging. An innocent remark can quickly turn into a major quarrel, ruining friendships as well as your lesson plan. Some pre-emptive measures:

- Create clear ground rules for group work before the activity. Each class can create their own rules and display these visually

- Think carefully about group dynamics. Team up pupils who have SLCN with peers who model good social communication skills

- Give every group member a clear role and something to do (notetaker, encourager, questioner, timekeeper)

- Praise and assess group working skills explicitly: *'Jason, you listened very carefully to others and asked when you didn't understand'*

- Identify what they could do to improve: *'Bethany, next time how could you ensure that everybody in the group contributes their ideas?'*

Group work rules!

Here are the rules and responsibilities one Year 9 class agreed for a group task about human rights.

Our Rules
Let people finish talking
Don't swear
Don't tell people they are wrong
Respect others
Listen to others
Say when you don't understand
Everybody shares the work
Don't shout
Help others

Jobs
Jason – write down everybody's ideas.
Cejay – encourage everybody to join in and give their ideas.
Britney – read out the questions and check all the tasks are done.
Joanne – fill in the task board.
Mazeem – make sure everybody stays on task.

 TIP! Present or refer to the rules at the beginning of *every* session, as pupils with SLCN often struggle to remember and generalise rules.

Peer feedback

Giving accurate and constructive feedback to peers can be difficult for children with social communication difficulties. They may come across as blunt, unfeeling or offensive. All children will benefit from being taught communication skills explicitly. The following approaches work well:

1. Providing a set formula; for instance a *'what went well'* followed by an *'even better if…'*
2. Giving pupils sentence starters to complete, eg: *What I like about your work is….*, *Next time maybe you could try…*
3. For pupils who struggle with 1. and/ or 2. supply a bank of sentences they can choose from with symbols or pictures to support.
4. Model how to give feedback appropriately or ask some pupils who have done this well to share it with the class.

Make sure pupils also understand how to receive feedback and use it constructively. They might need time with an adult to facilitate this.

Go out and play!

Pupils with social communication difficulties are likely to find unstructured times during the school day problematic. There is often no routine, a set of 'unwritten' rules to follow, and less adult supervision. Pupils who cope reasonably well in class may not cope at break and lunch times. *'Go outside and play'* is not so easy for these pupils. They find they have to:

- Make and maintain friendships
- Chat to other pupils
- Join in games and activities
- Negotiate and compromise
- Deal with 'falling out' and misunderstandings
- Understand jokes, idioms, sarcasm and teasing
- Behave in a 'socially acceptable' way
- Understand the unwritten social rules (such as not telling on friends, compromising or softening a response to avoid giving offence, etc.)
- Deal with peer pressure

Get the rulebook out

Provide clear rules, boundaries and expectations even during social times.

A group of Year 8 boys was in trouble every day for arguments that began during lunch time football matches and spilled over into afternoon lessons. They accused each other of cheating, changing the rules, pushing, taking over the game, and unfair teams. With the help of a teacher, the boys looked up the 'official' rules of football. They also agreed rules about selecting teams, taking turns in goal and what to do if things got out of hand. The lunch time football matches improved. One boy noted 'It's better now that everybody knows the same rules and how to sort out disagreements'.

How else can you support?
* Direct pupils to structured activities such as sports or homework clubs
* Make sure there are always quiet activities available such as books, computers, board games or art materials
* Ensure that everyone knows where to go for help or if they need 'time out'
* Some schools provide 'break time buddies', especially for students who are new to the school or shy and isolated

How can we teach 'social communication'?

It's one thing to know the 'hot spots' for students with weak social communication skills, but what can you do to help them develop the skills they lack? The next few pages look at how you can foster emotional literacy and conversational skills and how to repair communication breakdowns.

Social Skills Groups
Some schools run specific social communication groups for pupils with difficulties in this area. There are many commercial resources available which can help to structure such groups. You might like to try working on a different skill each session (eg: initiating/ joining/ ending a conversation, active listening, body language, tone of voice, making friends, giving and receiving compliments, being assertive, etc.) You will find some resources listed at the end of this book and, on page 127, an example of a typical social skills session.

Running a social skills group

Key points to consider when running a social communication skills group:

- When should the sessions take place? Pupils may resent being taken out of their favourite lesson each week!
- Think about the number of students in the group. Two is not enough for games and activities; more than seven or eight can mean a lot of 'waiting' time
- Make the sessions interesting and specific to the pupils in the group. Do they have interests or hobbies you can tap into? Would they respond well to clips from popular television programmes, eg to analyse feelings and body language?
- Break it up. The best social communication groups do not rely on worksheets. Use a mixture of discussion, role play, photo stories and video
- Make it relevant. A social communication skills group is not effective in isolation. Link every activity with what the pupils do in other situations. Encourage pupils to use the skills they learn over the next week and report back on what works. They might like to keep a tally chart or journal of their successes
- Include some good role models, perhaps pupils who need a safe environment to make friends, but who have good social skills

Social stories and comic strip conversations

Social stories and comic strip conversations are other useful methods of exploring social situations with pupils. Both were originally created by Carol Gray in the early 1990's as ways of teaching social skills to people with autism.

Social Stories are descriptions of particular events, situations or activities which show people what to expect in that situation.

Comic strip conversations are simple representations of all the 'levels' in a conversation. Stick drawings or cartoons may be used, with speech bubbles to show what is said, thought bubbles to show what people's intentions might be, and colour to denote their feelings.

You might want to seek training in these methods to learn how to use them effectively with your students.

Further reading: *My Social Stories Book*. C. Gray & A.L. White, 2002.

Social communication in the classroom

There are plenty of ways to teach and reinforce social communication skills in everyday classroom activities:

- Point out and praise positive use of such skills, (*Jenny, that was an excellent way of joining the conversation without interrupting.'*)

- Pause videos clips and DVDs to promote discussion about these skills – how are different characters feeling? How do we know this? What does their body language say? How have they started and ended conversations? Are they showing different levels of formality in different situations?

- Use drama activities and role plays. 'Freeze' the action and ask other pupils to comment on body language, facial expression and the language that has just been used. How could it be made more appropriate to the situation? How could they make their language more or less formal?

Feelings and emotions

Many children with SLCN find it difficult to identify and explain how they are feeling. Identifying and labelling emotions is one of the first steps in gaining 'emotional literacy' and is important for personal wellbeing as well as developing relationships with others.

How are you feeling? Happy, sad, angry, disgusted, afraid, surprised, greedy, jealous, rejected, accepted, excited, alienated, proud, confused, frustrated, loved, bored, betrayed, annoyed, lonely ……

There is a wealth of opportunity in English, Drama, PSHE, History, Geography, RE and tutor time to teach and extend vocabulary around emotions. Pupils won't learn emotions just by matching words to faces; they will need to discuss various situations and events and link these to their own experiences.

Case Study

An RE teacher asked pupils to fill in thought bubbles on a photo of civil rights activist Rosa Parks and other passengers on the bus. How did Rosa Parks feel? How did the other people on the bus feel? She then asked pupils to explain their thinking and relate it to other times they have experienced similar emotions.

The art of conversation

Although pupils may be very good at talking, they might need explicit work on how to hold an effective conversation. Asking pupils to create conversations or dialogues can help to revise subject content as well as improving conversational skills. Pupils could be assessed by peers using a checklist.

- English, History or Drama: two characters discuss a given theme or event
- RE or PSHE: pupils argue for or against a point of view
- Science: interview with a famous scientist
- Art or Music: pupils discuss a painting or piece of music

A conversational checklist

Remember to:
- Begin the conversation
- Consider body language
- Ask questions
- Answer questions
- Follow up answers
- Take turns
- Make relevant comments to show you were listening
- Move the conversation on
- End the conversation

Dealing with communication breakdowns

Inevitably there will be times when pupils with SLCN have breakdowns in communication. They may need to be shown what other people were thinking, or how their behaviour led to various consequences.

Ben likes acting and finds it useful to make photo stories or videos showing different situations. With the help of an adult he then identifies 'what went wrong' and role plays alternative responses or rehearses what he could do differently next time.

Daisy is very artistic. She draws cartoon strips and makes animations of social situations. An adult then encourages her to add in captions, speech and thought bubbles to identify what other people were thinking, feeling and doing. This helps her to see other people's point of view and identify her own emotions.

Some pupils enjoy making storyboards identifying what they did and the consequences of their actions. With the help of an adult they then consider alternative behaviours and what subsequent events might then have been.

A Whole School Approach

A school audit

Is your school 'communication-friendly'? You might like to carry out an audit of your school, department or classroom. You can find examples of audits and checklists at the Communication Trust and AFASIC, as well as from some of the other organisations listed in the resources section at the back of this book. You could start by looking at these three areas:

1. **How easy is it for a visitor or new pupil to find their way around?**

   - Is there clear, colour-coded signage?

   - Are signs backed up with visual support such as photos, pictures or symbols?

   - Are staff photos and names displayed on classrooms and offices?

A school audit

2. Is information for pupils visual and accessible?

- Are notices and important information at eye-level?
- Are classroom expectations and rules written in pupil-friendly language with visual back-up?
- Are there visual timetables for the school day, extra-curricular activities and events taking place this week/ month/ term?
- Are cupboards and trays containing equipment clearly labelled?
- Are key words displayed around the classroom, on the board or provided on paper with visual support?
- Are classrooms labelled clearly with information about staff and subject if appropriate?

A school audit

3. **Do pupils have alternative ways of recording and sufficient language support?**
   - Are worksheets clear and easy to follow?
   - Is reading material, including websites pupils are directed to, at a suitable reading age?
   - Are pupils shown finished examples of work?
   - Are clear and consistent instructions for homework provided?
   - Are pupils encouraged to seek clarification and to state when they do not understand?
   - Do pupils have access to alternative ways of recording, such as dictaphones, voice-text software or scribes?
   - Do pupils have access to talking dictionaries, spell checkers and calculators?

Effective collaboration with home

Effective collaboration with parents and carers is key to supporting pupils with SLCN. For pupils with memory, organisation and sequencing difficulties, relaying a message, getting started on homework or explaining what has happened that day can be an almost impossible task. The following systems work:

- Regular opportunities for parents to come into school
- Using the school text messaging system to send information about trips and special events
- Using a home-school book or organiser to write messages to parents
- Using your school's VLE to ensure parents have access to the calendar, letters home, school rules and homework

Don't forget to use parents' expertise. Ask them what strategies work at home and what their child's interests are outside of school. Insider knowledge can be invaluable!

Supporting pupils with homework

You can support parents of children with SLCN to help their child with homework by:

- Ensuring the child has clear, written instructions to take home, perhaps on a print-out or sticker
- Ensuring pupils have all the information and equipment they need, such as exercise books, text books, worksheets and lists of key vocabulary
- Allowing pupils to complete work in alternative ways, eg recording a speech instead of writing an essay
- Giving pupils plenty of time – some may need to wait until an adult is available to support them
- Encouraging pupils to use homework clubs before or after school or during lunch time
- Sharing your knowledge and resources. Tell parents about free online resources, websites or software that help their child in school

Working with teaching assistants

TAs can support pupils with SLCN in numerous ways. You might like to ask them to:

- Prepare vocabulary lists and other visual materials for use in class
- Adapt the language that they use with pupils
- Share information about pupils with SLCN
- Support social communication during group work
- Support pupils' understanding by creating diagrams, drawings, cartoon strips or flow charts to help students to create a mental image of the language being used
- Ensure that pupils are using strategies consistently across subjects
- Act as a reader or scribe in class or in examinations
- Provide support for understanding and completing homework
- Encourage pupils to take responsibility for their learning and promote independence
- Support pupils' memory skills and organisation by using task boards
- Take part in joint planning to share resources and strategies

Working with other staff

Pupils with SLCN come into contact with many adults during their time at school and a holistic approach to cross-curricular planning will have enormous benefits for pupils. If you have a pupil with SLCN in your class you can support both them and other staff by:

- Ensuring lunch time staff are aware of the difficulties the pupil might face during social times

- Providing supply teachers, cover supervisors and trainee teachers with information about the pupil's difficulties and effective strategies to use

- Working with staff organising school trips and special events to make sure they are aware of any potential difficulties. Will there be a lot of listening? Is there group work involved? Will pupils be expected to follow instructions independently?

Working with the speech and language therapist

Most speech and language therapy services in the UK have an open referral system, which means that anybody can refer. However, if you have concerns about a pupil, your first step should be to speak to their parents and your school's SENCO.

Once a child is referred to a Speech and Language Therapist (SLT) they will be seen for an initial assessment, usually in school. The SLT will assess the pupil's needs and discuss these with parents and school staff. School staff will be given strategies and recommendations to use with the pupil, and some pupils may be referred for specialist input. The most successful outcomes are when school, home and the SLT work together to target a pupil's needs. The role of the SLT in schools can include:

- Assessing, observing and monitoring speech and language difficulties
- Working with pupils individually or in small groups
- Training and advising school staff on a particular child or type of difficulty
- Advising on suitable resources and strategies to use
- Attending review meetings

Useful organisations and websites

Language for Learning (provides training and resources for those working with young people with SLCN) www.languageforlearning.co.uk

AFASIC (supports parents and young people with SLCN) www.afasic.org.uk

The Communication Trust (a coalition of 50 voluntary and community organisations with expertise in SLCN and many free resources. The Trust also has a 'What Works' database of evidenced interventions which support children's speech, language and communication skills.) www.thecommunicationtrust.org.uk

I CAN (information service and resources about SLCN) www.ican.org.uk

NAPLIC (National association of professionals concerned with language impairment in children) www.naplic.org.uk

NASEN (UK organisation promoting the development of children and young people with any type of special educational need) www.nasen.org.uk

The British Stammering Association (information and resources for pupils, parents and teachers) www.stammering.org

Software and interactive resources

Widgit software (symbol-supported learning materials. *Writing with Symbols* and *Communicate in Print* are two useful tools for the classroom) www.widgit.com

WriteOnline (online writing tool with mindmapping facility, spell predictor and screen-reader facility) www.cricksoft.com/uk/products/writonline/default.aspx

Dragon (voice-to-text software, available on PCs and as an app) www.nuance.co.uk/dragon

Inspiration (A mind-mapping tool) www.inspiration.com

Lexion (A software programme which assesses pupils in various aspects of language and literacy and suggests suitable exercises and games for that pupil) www.lexion.co.uk

Phoneme Factory (a screening and intervention system for children, particularly targeting phonological awareness) available from: www.speech-therapy.org.uk/phoneme-factory

Speech Link and Language Link (screening packages for schools across the age range providing assessment and interventions) www.speechlink.info

Further reading and resources

Reading
Language for Learning in the Secondary School
by S. Hayden & E. Jordan. Routledge, 2012
Language for Learning: A practical guide for supporting pupils with language and communication difficulties across the curriculum
by S. Hayden & E. Jordan. Routledge, 2007
Supporting Speech, Language and Communication Needs
by K. Ripley & J. Barrett. Sage publications, 2008

Resources
Talkabout - series of books (by A. Kelly). Programmes of work and activities to assess, teach and develop social communication skills, self-awareness and self-esteem in young children and teenagers.
Language for Thinking (by A. Branagan & S. Parsons). A programme to develop thinking and reasoning skills at primary and lower secondary age. Published by Speechmark

Word Aware (by A. Branagan & S. Parsons). A whole school approach to vocabulary teaching. Published by Speechmark
Black Sheep Press – resources and apps for primary and secondary pupils covering topics, narrative, speech sounds, social communication and other aspects of language. www.blacksheeppress.co.uk

Appendix: Sample social skills group session

Page 108 introduced the idea of social skills groups. Below is an example:

Time and Date:	Objective: To understand why facial expression is important when we are talking and listening

Time and Date:
Wednesday
8.45-9.15

Location:
Quiet room off the library

Pupils:
Joshua, Grace, Sanjit, Anika
(All Year 7)

Resources:
Video clips and display screen. Feelings cards. Sentences written on cards. iPad or video camera

Objective: To understand why facial expression is important when we are talking and listening

Activities:

1. Facilitator shows video clips from some popular TV shows without sound. The scenes are paused and pupils explain how they think the characters are feeling, taking into account facial expression and body language (covered the previous week).

2. Charades game. Pupils take it in turns to pick up a 'feelings' card. They have to show that feeling through their facial expression. Who can guess correctly? How did they know?

3. Silly sentences game. Pupils take a feelings card along with a sentence to read aloud in that manner (eg 'I am so angry with you' in a 'cheerful' manner). What do they notice? What's wrong?

4. Pupils filmed taking part in a conversation about what they did at the weekend. The video is played back. Can they comment on their facial expression? Is it aiding what they are saying?

About the Authors

Victoria Mason

Victoria began her career as a mainstream secondary school teacher and then worked as a teacher of SEN before specialising in SLCN. She currently works as a specialist teacher in a large mainstream secondary school's Language Unit, one of the few secondary Language Units in the country. She trains staff to meet the needs of pupils with SLCN in mainstream classrooms and provides specialist input for pupils with SLCN.

Emela Milne

Emela is a qualified speech and language therapist with over 25 years' experience working with children and young people with SLCN. She has worked with children with SLCN in clinics and health centres, as well as in nursery, primary and secondary school settings. She is a clinical supervisor for student speech and language therapists and delivers training and INSET for school staff working with pupils with SLCN. She is currently a speech and language therapist in three mainstream primary and secondary schools, all of which have specialist Language Units.